COMPACT
CYMRU

Tryfan:
Biography of a Mountain

Simon Gwyn Roberts

Gwasg Carreg Gwalch

First published in 2023
© text & photos: Simon Gwyn Roberts

ISBN: 978-1-84524-519-1
Cover design: Eleri Owen

Published by Gwasg Carreg Gwalch,
12 Iard yr Orsaf, Llanrwst, Wales LL26 0EH
tel: 01492 642031
email: books@carreg-gwalch.cymru
website: www.carreg-gwalch.cymru

Photo credit Geraint Lewis-Evans: Pg 24, 58, 66, 80

*previous page: Cloud inversion from East Face;
below: Tryfan from Senior's Ridge;
opposite: Typical climbing on the East Face*

Contents

Introduction

Everybody can remember the first time. For the memory to be most indelible, it should be seared into the central core of your hippocampus by approaching from the east, rounding the corner into the Ogwen valley a mile or two after leaving Capel Curig. And there it is, unlike anything else in Wales: a serrated blade of rock, triple towered, looking every inch the proper mountain.

Continue west down Ogwen and the magic intensifies. Despite the array of fine mountains on all sides, the eyes always come to rest on it. The closer you get, the more impressive it is, rising from the base of the valley as a towering mass of granite. Get even closer, and you begin to pick out obvious features across the East Face as the mountain begins to cohere into something even more distinguished. A big ledge seems to cut the mountain in half. Three large but discrete buttresses become clear and distinctive, split by dark gullies. There is a weird symmetry to it all that holds the gaze.

There are also two figures on the summit – or are they large rock obelisks?

For most, certainly for anybody with even a dash of adventurous spirit in their bloodstream, it will be essential to get to the top as quickly as possible. It is such a compelling objective, only the very timid would be happy to leave it with the view from the valley.

And for most, it then becomes a firm favourite. It casts its spell on hillwalkers and climbers alike, and is often the mountain that outdoor enthusiasts have climbed most often. In my case, I first saw Tryfan as a young boy but didn't go up the North Ridge until I was a teenager. Since that day in the 1980s I've been up it at least a hundred times. I've slept on it, done all the scrambles, done all the classic rock climbs (bar one), dined on it, tried to run up it, attempted to run down it, tried to botanise on it.

It is more than just a mountain: it is a constant presence, a backdrop to life itself.

Tryfan is probably the most instantly recognisable peak in the British Isles. By that, I mean that its profile and general appearance means that almost any hill-goer would identify it immediately. Spreading the net as widely and impartially as possible, I would suggest that its only rivals for that title are An Teallach, Liathach, Suilven or Slioch in the north-west Highlands of Scotland. All four have distinctive profiles but all four are reserved for the more committed, well-travelled mountain enthusiast.

Perhaps Sgurr nan Gillean or Blaven on Skye might give Tryfan's profile a run for its money, and possibly Errigal in Donegal or Brandon on the Dingle peninsula. England's closest equivalent would probably be Great Gable in the Lakes, and Yr Wyddfa (Snowdon) might challenge it on home ground.

On balance, however, it is not too controversial to say that Tryfan wins – and, of course, it is far more accessible for most hillwalkers than those other contenders, and vastly more accessible to casual roadside observers. It also has more to offer. That is not a biased statement, merely an acknowledgement that Tryfan has something for everyone in a way that its 'rivals' do not: everything from simple scrambles to hard rock climbs, and everything in between those two extremes.

It also has to be said at the outset that it is quite hard to write about Tryfan without reverting to cliché. This book will

Approaching the West Face

try to avoid those clichés, but it is difficult. This is partly due to context. In the context of the British Isles, Tryfan is very special. You might not notice it if it was tucked away at the end of an Alpine valley or up in the far corner of Utah. But it isn't: it's here and it's ours. It is considerably more dramatic than most mountains in these gentle islands, and that rarity gives it a certain cachet, and a definite draw. This means that writers reach for superlatives – wild, epic, majestic and the like – more often than they should. Again, this book will try to resist that temptation, but suffice to say that Tryfan is a special peak and demands to be celebrated as such.

And although it is tempting to blame some of this UK-centric hyperbole on social media, there is nothing new here. When I first started walking and climbing in the Welsh hills in the 1980s, Walter Poucher's guidebooks were still the only thing available. Even then they were amusingly dated with their calls for nailed boots, 'close-woven tweed' and their observations that 'the feathered, velour Austrian hat is seldom seen nowadays'.

Although he would never have said 'epic' or 'awesome', Poucher's style was distinctive, with flowery and repetitive passages where the rock was 'furnished' with holds, crags were the 'treasured playground of rock gymnasts' and, in the case of his description of Tryfan's summit, 'on a sunny day it is usual to find a number of climbers gathered round this lofty perch; for it is a pleasant spot on which to eat lunch'. He cautions that the view encompasses 'the very tip of Snowdon which will be missed even on a clear day by those who do not possess an alert and discerning eye!' Seen from the north, 'one savage cwm follows another from east to west, all of them hemmed in by striking mural precipices'.

Language changes, the hyperbole continues, but that view remains the same, even if the 'striking mural precipices' are now 'epic cliffs'.

8   *Tryfan*

Tryfan's dramatic outline has always attracted artists;
Rob Piercy's image of Tryfan from Nant y Benglog

Origins

The name itself is a long-running bone of contention and a fertile topic for debate, and has been for many years. E.W. Steeple in Carr and Lister's 1948 '*Mountains of Snowdonia*' guidebook suggests it derives from 'try' (through) and 'ban' (peak). Hence, he suggests a translation approximating to 'the peak of the passage'. This seems rather unlikely. More likely seems some kind of derivation from 'tri faen' (the more prosaic 'three stones', given that the triple buttresses are the most obvious and notable feature of the mountain).

However, others dispute this and have suggested that 'try' might also be a modifier, an intensifying superlative. Therefore, under this interpretation of the name, 'try' means 'very', and 'fan' is a peak, as in the 'Carmarthen Fan' or 'Bannau Brycheiniog' (*Brecon Beacons*), hence 'Tryfan' means '*very* peaked or pointed'. Perhaps, although I would observe that 'fan' is uncommon in north Wales, and is much more common in the south. The two clause explanation for the name could also indicate a mountain rising high to a slender peak, depending on taste. It seems unlikely that the true meaning of Tryfan's name will ever be definitively settled to the exclusion of all other options.

Steeple (who was an English climber rather than an expert on local nomenclature) also quotes a stanza of the Verses of the Graves (*Englynion y Beddau*), perhaps the oldest written reference to the mountain's name, which states that (in Steeple's romanticised, flowery version) 'the grave of Bedwyr is in Gallt Tryfan... He is the Bedivere[1] of the idylls, who cast Arthur's sword into the lake, and watched the wounded monarch's barque glide into the distance 'till the hull look'd one black dot against the verge of dawn.'

On the subject of nomenclature, many of Tryfan's most well-known features were named by climbers or early tourists, and therefore still carry jarring, inappropriate English names. The 'Cannon', 'Heather Terrace' and 'Milestone Buttress' are all examples, as are the names of the climbs

---

[1] *Bedivere/Bedwyr was one of Arthur's knights: he is supposedly buried on Tryfan's flank, to simplify the rather overwrought translation.*

themselves (with some exceptions). This is unfortunate, but to be charitable it is at least a fairly logical upshot of earlier Victorian exploration and mentality. Climbers have always named their own routes, the first person to lead the route gets to name and grade it, and it is perhaps understandable that these have generally led to English names in the past, often highly inventive. This has changed to an extent in recent years, and there has been an effort to rename certain features (for example, Heather Terrace to Llwybr Gwregys – although some authorities claim the correct, and original, name for this feature is actually Llwybr Llechan Goch [Red Rock Path]).

Much more serious is the creeping Anglicisation of the landscape itself, the renaming of key topographical features that are known to all (not just a few rock climbers) and have always had Welsh names. The worst, most infamous example is the tendency to call Llyn Bochlwyd, 'Lake Australia', in misguided reference to its shape. The seriousness of the implications of this are hard to overstate and the issue is now thankfully getting a degree of wider publicity.

Llyn Bochlwyd (meaning *grey cheek*, a perfect description) is the subject of many photographs from Tryfan's summit, nestling in the cwm below, framed by the crags of Glyder Fach and y Gribin, and of course named centuries before Australia was even discovered by Europeans, let alone mapped. It is almost too obvious to spell out the significance of this, but if we lose reference to place, we lose something fundamental and irreplaceable about our heritage.

A topographical primer

Returning to the weird symmetry of Tryfan, in the middle of the East Face sits the impressive Central Buttress: which is particularly imposing when viewed from the Capel Curig direction. This perhaps is the best and most logical starting point for a summary of the mountain's topography, which is simultaneously beautifully simple and rather complex – in the sense that, looking at the peak from below, it appears straightforward, but it is often notoriously difficult to locate yourself once on the mountain itself.

Even the most recent climbing guidebook to Ogwen concedes this, despite all the advances in aerial photography and graphic design that help climbers and walkers identify and locate their chosen routes: 'The overall structure of the face appears fairly simple, as indeed it is, but this can be deceptive... the gullies and buttresses all look bafflingly alike, and helpful landmarks are notably few'.

To the left of the Central Buttress is the more elegant, less bulky South Buttress, the two separated by the well-defined South Gully. To the right is the North Buttress, almost as extensive as Central, from which it is separated by the deep North Gully, probably the most impressive gully line on the mountain. All three are underlined by the gently inclining shelf, clearly visible from the valley, known as the Heather Terrace/Llwybr Llechan Goch. Most of the climbs and scrambles start from the Terrace and wend their way up the buttresses.

To the right of the three main buttresses lie three smaller buttresses, which – although less important – are worth committing to memory as they help with the location of different routes and ridges. Green Gully and Nor'Nor' buttresses are divided by two eponymous gullies (Green and Nor'Nor', which is presumably a defunct Victorian way of saying 'furthest North'). Finally, the much smaller Bastow Gully bookends the first steep rock encountered from the A5 road below.

But it is not just the famous view from the East, because Tryfan has two faces and two sides. East and West. Sunny and

Tryfan from Ogwen

shady. Popular and unpopular. Morning and afternoon. Yin and yang.

The Western side of the mountain, as seen from Ogwen Cottage, is considerably less elegant and on first acquaintance less impressive. It has some interesting scrambles and long mountaineering routes – and it also offers the fastest, most direct route to the summit for fell runners and other unhinged individuals. It looks rather broken, but it still has a great deal of bare rock, it still attracts the attention from the West, and it still stands out amidst its neighbours. It catches the afternoon and evening sun, and is a perfect counterpoint to the more basic appeals of the East Face – an attractive location for the connoisseur and the seeker of solitude.

One area of the Western face is very well known, however, and that is the Milestone Buttress just above the A5 – which has been a motoring landmark for decades. It is named after the tenth milestone from Bangor, and the old sign, which reads 'Holyhead 35, Bangor 10, C. Curig 4', in an archaic script, is still there, built into the wall beside the road.

Climbing on the Milestone Buttress has a very long history, almost as long as any crag in the British Isles, partly as a result of its obviousness, its accessibility and its relative gentleness. Some of its routes were pioneered by the legendary London Welshman Owen Glynne Jones (the 'only genuine' Jones, as he styled himself) and popularised by a report of an ascent by the Abraham brothers in 1904, which was supposedly enlivened by an encounter with a decomposing dead sheep at a critical point, half way up.

Tony Moulam, writing in the 1956 climbing guidebook, referred to the extreme popularity and fame of the buttress: 'Perhaps there is no need to describe the position of the rocks. They are known to most people who find themselves in North Wales. Photographs have appeared in the national and motoring press and there is even a novel called *Murder on the Milestone Buttress*.'[2]

Further to the east, in the Capel Curig direction, lies Tryfan Bach ('*little Tryfan*'), a tiny facsimile of its near neighbour. Its general aspect is reversed, however, as it is the West facing slab that attracts most attention. This is a broad, superficially impressive sweep of very clean rock, scoured and polished by decades of attention from novice rock climbers. As with the Idwal Slabs in nearby Cwm Idwal, with which it shares some similarities, it is not always ideal for the purpose to which it has been assigned for many years, that of climbing nursery. It is disconcertingly polished, for one thing, and frequently crowded, for another.

A little to the west, and hidden from view, is an even smaller Tryfan, unknown to most. This is Tryfan Bychan ('smallest

---

[2] *The superbly named Shakespearean actor Abercrombie Lewker 'turns detective when a member of his climbing party is killed on what was supposed to be an easy route on a mountain in Wales'. The book was first published in the US, with its UK edition published in 1951.*

Tryfan'), another west-facing slab, but this time only ten metres high. With this, that weird triple symmetry of the mountain emphasised by its three giant buttresses shows itself again. Like Russian dolls, the valley contains three different Tryfans, each one smaller than the one before.

I feel certain that if you looked hard enough in the land beyond Tryfan Bychan, you might find a 'micro Tryfan', or even a 'nano Tryfan', a tiny rock shaped like the dominant peak: it would be rather satisfying, geology as high art.

No account of Tryfan's topography would be complete without a brief mention of the 'Cannon', the obvious rock feature on the North Ridge which marks the point at which several microroutes

Cannon with Y Garn beyond

Cloud inversion from East Face

converge and the ridge itself coalesces into something more coherent and defined. As previously mentioned, its English name is inappropriate and unfortunate, and tends as a result to attract the attention of English visitors for whom it is easy to pronounce and remember, rather like the nearby 'Cantilever' on Glyder Fach. To be fair, however, there has never been (as far as I am aware) an indigenous name for the Cannon (unlike the Cantilever, which is Y Gwyliwr in Welsh – The Sentinel).

Another example of the same phenomenon is the '*Castle of the Winds*', merely the literal English translation of '*Castell y Gwynt*', that well known rock feature between Glyder Fawr and Glyder Fach. I mention this because, whilst writing this book, I happened to be walking up Y Garn with my son Morgan. Just below Twll Du/Devil's Kitchen, we found ourselves stuck below a group of six young men struggling up one of the rocky steps that characterise this particular path, all of whom were clearly new to the mountain environment.

'Are we heading in the right direction?' they asked, an increasingly common question in these GPS-dependent days, to which there is only one possible non-patronising response: 'It depends where you want to go'. The answer to that was something I hadn't anticipated: 'We're heading for the Castle of the Winds'. It is obvious why this might attract the attention of visiting English tourists, but I had never really thought of it as a 'destination' before, not least because it isn't really a summit: it doesn't mark the highpoint of anything in particular, but it does have a wonderfully romantic name, which can be readily translated into the Germanic tongue.

The more I thought about this, the more obvious it became: there are very few features in Snowdonia that have English names, or even English translations. Those that do become fixated upon by a certain kind of visitor. My son then told me that his old scout leader had coined his own digestible neologism for Moel Wnion in the northern Carneddau. Almost unbelievably, it was, to him, 'the onion'. This was too barbaric for my mind to contemplate, so we moved on.

The summit

The twin monoliths that poke out of the jumbled summit rocks have been known as 'Adam and Eve' for a very long time. It seems an almost inevitable coinage, given their appearance from Ogwen and the frequency with which biblical references occur in the landscape (some of which are considerably more obscure, and would be lost on most people nowadays). In Welsh, they are known as 'Adda ac Efa' (again, the literal translation) or 'Siôn a Siân', although this does seem a somewhat more recent coinage.

In the context of the British Isles, there is no other summit with such a startling natural twin feature on the summit. The Inaccessible Pinnacle on Skye overtops its parent peak (Sgurr Dearg) but also dwarfs it, while the Cantilever/Y Gwyliwr, nearby on Glyder Fach is equally startling. But there are no other summits with double monoliths like this. For true comparisons, you have to look elsewhere – the Svolvaer Goat on the Lofoten Islands of Norway, for example. On that peak, climbers make the leap between the two giant 'goat' horns whilst looking directly down to the Svolvaer town cemetery, 1000 feet below their feet. The leap between Adam and Eve, and back again, is not quite that dramatic, but it does focus the mind and really should be left to the confident as you will hurt yourself badly if you miss, very badly if you miss on the eastern side.

Completing the leap earns you 'the freedom of Tryfan', although what that actually means has never been clear. It sounds an attractive concept, and unlike its urban equivalent is nicely democratic, depending only on one's inner fortitude for completion, rather than an obsequious blessing from local bigwigs. I remember reading many years ago of a Tryfan devotee in earlier times who arranged his own 'freedom of Tryfan' by spending years preparing and hiding little stashes of food and drink in various obscure nooks and crannies across the mountain. His idea (and I am pretty sure it was a man) was that these private stashes would enable him to spend more time on his favourite peak, to give him some additional flexibility for his lifelong exploration.

We are now a little more enlightened, and stashing food does not seem a very environmentally friendly way of celebrating the mountain. Pack it in, pack

it out: the standard advice applies to Tryfan as much as anywhere else in the Welsh mountains. Sustainability, and the fairly obvious ability to look after yourself, is key. There is no obvious water source on the mountain itself, although rivulets form in various places during the all-too-frequent spells of wet weather. Unlike Snowdon, of course, there is no mechanised way up, there is no café waiting for you at the summit – and this

may further explain its appeal to the outdoors community.

Despite the lack of a café, or train, you will rarely have the summit to yourself. On a sunny summer's day, it is common to see scores of people up here. Fortunately, although the summit is small by Snowdonian standards, it is still pretty

Y Garn from the summit

commodious, and there are plenty of nooks and crannies in which to enjoy a relatively private picnic. To avoid the crowds, the usual advice applies. Either be imaginative in your choice of route, or with the time of day, or with the time of year. It is worth noting, however, that Tryfan's lure is nowadays exerted all year round. It is an increasingly rare treat to have the summit to yourself.

I slept on the summit once, in the late 1980s with my friend Steven Jones. I never did it again, as it's not the most comfortable perch. Finding a piece of flat ground for a relaxing bivouac is challenging. But we were young, with an unusually high tolerance of discomfort; standard bivvy equipment in those days being a large orange polythene bag into which you inserted your sleeping bag and then waited for litres of condensation to form and pour onto your face. It was atmospheric dozing on the summit, but nothing out of the usual, until the early hours – perhaps around 2am – when we were both woken by a remarkably strange 'sonic boom', which shook the mountain (and our internal organs). It seemed to come from everywhere at once, from above and below, a very deep rumbling explosion.

To this day, neither of us is entirely sure what this was. At the time, Concorde was still flying – so it might have been that. Or a meteor entering the atmosphere. Alternatively, it might have been

Bochlwyd from the summit

North Tower from the summit

connected to the quarries in Bethesda, not too far away. I like to think of myself as a rational person, as does Steve, so more fanciful notions have rarely been entertained. Occasionally, however, it is hard not to indulge, as the mist swirls around, dusk starts to fall, and the grey granite boulders melt in and out of view; at such times the summit becomes a very different place from the usual crowded platform replete with sandwich-eating walkers, conversation and laugher. A sonic boom then feeds our more primitive instincts, it becomes an inexplicable, unsettling phenomenon. You can see how myths are born.

I asked Steve for his memories about the incident, as I don't remember discussing it much in recent years (he now lives in Pembrokeshire). 'It definitely happened', he said. 'It felt like a deep resonating boom from deep within the ground. I did wonder if it was to do with "Electric Mountain" but it was real and weird and I've never experienced anything like it since.'

As with all lower summits, wherever you are in the world, the view from Tryfan is much better than the kind of 'helicopter' views you tend to get from higher peaks. Whereas the likes of Snowdon, Ben Nevis or Everest give you a giant vista, a bird's eye view, this is rarely as spectacular or photogenic as being on a lower mountain surrounded by peaks of a similar stature. Almost all the most memorable views I have experienced, those I look back on as I drift off to sleep each night, fit this 'lower' criteria.

In Tryfan's case, your eye will probably first be drawn by the cwms and ridges of the nearby Glyderau, the 'striking mural precipices' lauded by Walter Poucher. There is a lot of rock here, from the fine Main Cliff on Glyder Fach round to the more broken gullies that give nice winter climbs on Y Garn. To the right, the verdant Nant Ffrancon stretches down towards Bethesda with the Menai Strait and Anglesey beyond. Perhaps, on a clear day, you might see further down the Llyn.

Closer at hand, the Carneddau loom above the North Tower, the final obstacle on the ridge, something you have probably just negotiated, or circumvented. Across the deep gulf of the Ogwen Valley rises Pen yr Olau Wen, with the rest of the range stretching out beyond, their broad undulations very different in character to the rocky Glyderau. To the east, the view rolls down to Moel Siabod, the Moelwynion and beyond as Eryri gives way to Hiraethog, the Clwydians, Migneint and the uplands of mid Wales.

If you are lucky enough to be up here on one of those early summer evenings of great clarity, you will notice the pattern of the land, the way in which little knolls and tiny crags suddenly become visible as they are illuminated by the soft light of the setting sun. The glacial history of the valleys radiating out from the summit becomes even more obvious as the shadows fall, particularly the over-deepened valley of Nant Ffrancon stretching down towards Anglesey.

over: Tryfan from across Llyn Idwal

The scrambles

In geological terms, Tryfan is the easternmost limb of an upfold, the compliment of the Idwal syncline. The upward arching of the rock strata can be seen in the backwall of Cwm Tryfan. According to Millward and Robinson's 'Landscapes of North Wales', the double fold of Cwm Idwal and Cwm Tryfan involving Ordovician beds 'provides a clear illustration of the way in which the various rock types have been compressed into a number of subsidiary folds within the major regional syncline of Snowdonia.' The East Face was created by the tendency of lavas to break off along vertical contraction-joints, and that same jointing effect is also the reason for the two stones of Adam and Eve on the summit.

With the sun low in the sky, the columnar rocks common on Tryfan and the rest of the Glyderau can be fully appreciated. The shadows and strangely symmetrical shapes are due to the natural splitting of rocks that have been subjected to intense heat and pressure millennia ago. This splitting or jointing leaves smooth faces, but also useful cracks from a climbing perspective.

This is all rather dry and technical (which is why I have quoted it from another source) but an appreciation of basic geology becomes second nature to climbers and scramblers, who quickly learn to distinguish different rock types and may well find themselves physically better suited to limestone, perhaps, or Peak District grit. Different rock types tend to require different physical attributes: slate, for example, is often about delicate, precise footwork on tiny edges. By contrast, gritstone tends to suit the more thuggish, squat, powerful climber.

Tryfan, however, is something of a law unto itself. It is a huge chunk of prime Welsh granite, but its characteristic triple structure lends the buttresses individual identity, and the frequent ledges and large, juggy holds (often hidden from below) make climbing on it a relaxing delight. Here are Millward and Robinson again, getting to the geological specifics of what makes Tryfan unique: 'The main mass of the mountain is formed of a succession of lava flows separated by beds of shale, a combination of rocks which give it a distinctive character and appearance. The lava has a tendency to break off along contraction joints and this can give rise to columns of rock, like the 'two stones' of the summit, often mistakenly taken for climbers'.

This all means that Tryfan is a mountain built for scrambling. It is famous for its easy mountaineering rock climbs, and we will come to those later, but what it really provides in glorious abundance is scrambling. Wonderful, uncluttered, unencumbered scrambling – the kind of mountain terrain that hovers somewhere between walking and proper climbing.

There are multiple definitions, but actually 'scrambling' (as it is generally defined in Britain) replicates in miniature the kind of mountain movement you will often encounter in bigger ranges like the Alps, Pyrenees, Tatra or Corsica. Not technically difficult, rarely requiring a rope for the confident and competent, emphasising complete freedom of movement, but potentially the most serious and dangerous form of mountaineering because of the terrain, and the obvious fact that you may well go a long way if you fall off unroped.

Tryfan has a lot of this. The most famous of all is the North Ridge, alongside Crib Goch (and Striding Edge on Helvellyn) the most well-known and frequented scramble in the whole of Wales, and probably Britain. It starts just above the A5 itself. Park your car, climb a few steps, move to the left a bit, and you're on it – a sustained series of obstacles, never too serious, never particularly hard.

The North Ridge can be rather confusing, however, particularly at the bottom where it isn't much of a ridge at all. So many routes and paths have been beaten out over so many years that it is very common to see aspirants standing in little groups, staring upwards with a confused look on their faces, perhaps with map or guidebook in hand, trying in vain to identify features.

Often, people head upwards too early, only to return with tail between legs having discovered a tricky wall or two. The most ancient ropeless climbing advice would be appropriate here: don't climb up what you can't climb down. One particularly infamous hazard here is the wet cleft known as Waterfall Gully, a good illustration of the hazards that lurk, particularly for those that choose to descend the ridge.

Two figures on the North Ridge

In fact, the best route heads leftwards (east) for quite some time and only then kicks upwards onto the ridge itself. Above, after some tricky sections, the ridge (still broad) eases in angle and gradually becomes more defined before it reaches its first famous and unmissable feature: the Cannon.

As we have already established, the Cannon is a jutting prow of rock visible from the valley below (particularly from the Ogwen cottage direction). We will return to it again later, but for now suffice to say that it acts reassuringly to mark the onward route. Whether you choose to slither up it or not for a photograph is entirely up to you – as is the optional direct scramble up from the Cannon, a grade two variation that feels harder. From here, the standard ridge is a delight, short level sections giving way to enjoyable (and usually optional) rock work.

One major obstacle remains, the North Tower, often mistaken for the main summit when seen from below. It is, as its name suggests, rather intimidating – although as is so often the case with this friendly mountain, appearances are deceptive. In fact, it unfolds quite logically and the tricky direct ascent can be bypassed either by the standard enjoyable gully (a little further right), a grassy traverse path above the east face, or by easier scrambling to the west, although this does require a lot of care to avoid difficult ground.

After this comes a memorable and atmospheric (particularly in mist) moment when the route descends into a pronounced narrow col. In the Alps, this would be called a breche. Here, it is known as the notch and – like the cannon – is very obvious from the west. In my view it is one of the most atmospheric micro-places in the Welsh mountains. It lends its name to the gloriously simple arête that joins it from the west face below, which we will return to in the climbing chapter.

The concept of 'first ascents' of summits is somewhat alien in the context of the UK, where the vast majority of mountains would have been climbed by shepherds, farmers and probably even early hunter gatherers for practical reasons (retrieving sheep, establishing defensive viewpoints and the like). However, given its intimating appearance and relative difficulty it seems unlikely that the North Ridge was frequently ascended until the eighteenth century or perhaps the early Victorian era. In fact, it was included in early climbing guides as an 'easy course' under the original British adjectival climbing grading system (easy, moderate, difficult), conceived by the aforementioned Owen Glynne Jones.

Nowadays, the North Ridge sits firmly in scrambling guidebooks, regarded as a 'grade one', an entry level taste of real mountaineering for thousands, and a gateway drug into something bigger and more addictive for others. As Jim Perrin says of Tryfan in his *Hills of Wales*, 'no wonder that generation upon generation of hillgoers have extended their allegiance from walking to climbing on this very peak. It suggests to you that to climb is as easy and natural a thing as the act of walking itself'.

Most of the other scrambles on Tryfan are harder. There are a few exceptions, two of which are little known and perhaps deserve a wider audience. The first of these is the 'direct route', which has in recent times become quite popular among fell runners as a classic speed test. The direct is hardly likely to appeal to the average hill-walker, however, as it slogs up the grass and scree chutes on the western side of the mountain before making a beeline for the western gully, a shattered, polished route well-known to anybody who has ever done the Welsh 3000s in the standard way. It isn't really a scramble until that final gully, but it is horribly steep throughout.

When I first started visiting Ogwen in the 1980s, I seem to remember most people still took the 'trade route' up to the Heather Terrace, walked all the way along this to the stile at Bwlch Tryfan, and then turned right to head up the South Ridge. This remains, perhaps, the easiest route in the sense that you very rarely have to get to grips with the rock. But it is far less direct (decidedly indirect, in fact) and infinitely less satisfying than the North Ridge. Bingley gives an early description of climbing Tryfan from Cwm Bochlwyd, presumably by the same South Ridge, in which 'we could scarcely take half a dozen steps together in any place without at the same time using our hands'.

Reverend Bingley was the botanist who recorded what is often cited as the first Welsh rock climb, up the Eastern Terrace of Clogwyn du'r Arddu on the dark flanks of Snowdon. He wrote about it in 'A tour round north Wales', a very early 1798 account of the Welsh mountain landscape and the sort of early tourism it inspired. The Heather Terrace remains a lovely route though, even if it is convoluted. It is steep lower down too, particularly when it leaves the boggy valley to head upwards in earnest.

This leads to a broad gully and an area that I was once told mountain rescuers refer to as Piccadilly Circus, as it marks the vague point where the Heather Terrace reaches one of the possible lines up the North Ridge: it tends to be crowded as a result, and it also has a slightly tricky traverse at the top that leads to the start of the Terrace proper.

Less well known as an ascent route, yet something of a hidden gem, is the

combination of Little and North Gullies on the dramatic East Face. From below, this looks intimidating, but it is by far the easiest way up the East Face – perhaps just a tad harder than the North Ridge itself, although there isn't much in it. It is also the easiest way down the face, and as such is a very useful piece of knowledge to have in your armoury, particularly if you aspire

East Face

to the famous climbs hereabouts: committing it to memory is a good idea, as you really don't want to continue down North Gully, which contains awkward chockstones and is definitely not suitable.

It is one of my favourite ways up, leaving the Heather Terrace just after the deep, dark cleft of the North Gully to take a series of steep little rises up the narrow Little Gully. It eases soon afterwards and then moves rightwards into the simple top section of North Gully before weaving southwards to pop out at Adam and Eve.

For many years, I laboured under the misapprehension that I (a climber and fell runner of very modest ability) held the secret to the much-vaunted 'quickest way' up the mountain by this route. I made numerous attempts, trying different micro-lines and tiny short-cuts. In reality, however, I was quite wrong. The quickest way up the mountain from the A5 road (which seems the logical starting point for the small group of deranged fell runners interested in such things) is certainly the aforementioned direct line which heads straight up the steep grass and scree below the west face. There is a narrow but distinctive path which is (unsurprisingly) relentlessly steep, but also relentlessly direct. Where the angle eases a tad, it heads left for the first open gully which joins the north ridge just below the top.

The record, which will probably be hard to believe for those outside the fell running community, currently stands at 28 minutes from road to summit, at least according to Strava, a running and cycling app which records GPS times for standardised 'segments'. The best I have managed is a rather more pedestrian 34 minutes.

The record for the fell runners' descent, by the way, is considerably more remarkable – and no doubt even harder for ordinary hill goers to believe. Mike Blake, who organises a unique fell race (called the Tryfan Downhill Dash) which takes this same direct route *down* the mountain every August, is said to have made the road from the summit in eight minutes flat. According to the current Strava segment (again, not necessarily the most accurate way of measuring these things – and certainly not as accurate as the records from a properly timed race), the current record for the descent stands at just under eight minutes.

There are other scrambles on both sides of the mountain. Most languish in obscurity, although that is a fairly relative notion on Tryfan. The South Buttress is one such, wending its way up spiky ribs and heathery gullies. The nearby South Gully is another, a reasonably well-defined route up the eponymous and unmistakeable feature.

A gully, in mountaineering terms, is a deep vertical rift in the rock – they were popular as routes of ascents in the earliest days of climbing as they give a veneer of security. They are usually damp and dark places, for obvious reasons, and are rarely frequented nowadays, although there are always a handful of unhinged enthusiasts that enjoy them, and some are still regarded as classics.

The huge Great Gully on Craig yr Ysfa is the most celebrated Welsh example, a memorable experience for any mountaineer. By contrast with that famous climb, South Gully is not a classic, but it is a nice route up Tryfan, and also acts as a helpful landmark, separating as it does the Central and South Buttress of the mountain. It can act as a useful descent, but only for competent climbers.

There are also scrambles up the Central and North Buttresses, and shorter scrambles further north on the lower Bastow and Nor'Nor' buttresses (these are the chunks of rock seen on the right, gradually descending in order of height from the three main buttresses). Nor'Nor' gully itself houses a nice and fairly easy route – not up the gully itself, which contains a few nasty surprises – but up a line of grooves (shallow open corners) on its left-hand side. This is known as Nor'Nor' groove and is another grade one or two scramble worth seeking out on busy days as an alternative to the crowded North Ridge.

On the Western side of the mountain lurk even more options for the scrambler or explorer determined to avoid the crowds. The best of these is probably the aforementioned Notch Arete, which is a delightful ascent hovering somewhere between a scramble and a very easy rock climb – it heads up beautiful golden granite to the eponymous 'notch' and is well seen from the vicinity of Ogwen cottage.

Notch Arete has something of an Alpine feel about it. It is easy angled and very simple, but the perfect granite glows gold as it catches the evening sunshine, which it often does – along with the rest of the Western side of Tryfan. I have introduced at least three people to the delights of rock climbing on this route: in my view, it is more suitable than lots of other routes used for that purpose, although it is admittedly a tad too easy, even for first-timers. It is also a very long haul from the road, which is a more pertinent drawback.

Lower down, and providing a suitable preliminary route with which to access the arête, lies an obvious Y shaped gully, again well seen from the vicinity of Ogwen cottage. Scrambles either side of the gully, or up it, provide access. To the left, the V-shaped buttress also has good scrambles up various lines. These are never quite as obvious when you are trying to locate them from directly below, but they are worth seeking out – and you certainly will not be queuing when you get there.

Lower down still, closer to the famous Milestone Buttress above the A5 (to which we will return in the climbing section) lies the Wrinkled Tower, which, in the words of Steve Ashton's iconic 1980s scrambling guide 'promises a great adventure – provided a route can be contrived among the clinging heather, cascading runnels and impossible towers'.

Ashton's book was something of a bible for my friends and I as we started our mountaineering journey in the 1980s. This route only appeared in the second edition, so we eagerly embraced it as soon as it was published. He notes that the 'faulty tower' that forms the exposed top section of this route 'lies at the upper limit of scrambling difficulty'. It does indeed, and I can still remember the exposed moves that gain a flake at the end of the sloping ramp that forms the top of the final tower. Again, it is worth stressing that all of this is far removed from both the sunny East Face on the other side of the mountain, and even the crowded Milestone Buttress, just below.

And these are just the better known scrambles. There are plenty more scattered around the mountain, some of which are very rarely ascended and retain an adventurous, pioneering feel.

Tryfan is, famously, the only mountain in 'Wales and England' or 'England and Wales' (a preposterous geographical designation, but one that we still seem to be stuck with) that you need to use your hands to get up. In other words, everything on the mountain qualifies as a scramble – just. As such, you remember the first time. For me, it was early summer 1988, a few weeks after my 18th birthday.

I didn't grow up in a mountaineering household, although with family from Penmachno I was very familiar with the Ogwen valley. I was, however, a curious teenager with a mildly adventurous streak, so went for a long weekend in Snowdonia, driving my nain's white 1960s mini, along with schoolfriends Tim, Rich and Steve

Ogwen from the West Face

from the Vale of Clwyd. They already knew the ropes, having embraced the outdoor pursuits wing of what was then called 'PE' while I tried in vain to play football, which was something of a family tradition. I was the neophyte, new to the mountain environment.

We camped at Gwern Gof Isaf, which to this day enjoys perhaps the best view of the East Face, looking straight up at it in all its glory. It is possible to discern most of the features of the mountain from this sheltered position in the bottom of the valley, and all of the best climbing lines are fairly obvious. Our objective on this first occasion was, of course, the North Ridge. It seemed intimidating, hard even, for me at the time in my raw recruit state.

From memory, I think we may have traversed Crib Goch the day before, going astray towards the top of Crib y Ddisgyl in the kind of warm summer mist that quickly becomes familiar to Welsh hillgoers. Again, from memory, I found that a troubling and novel experience, and was not keen to repeat it.

In the event, of course, it was tremendous fun and every one of these early experiences did a little more to light the blue touch paper, albeit incrementally. They embed themselves in your memory, and I can still remember that first trip up the North Ridge, playing around on the Cannon, and the view from the summit at the top: I can even recall my companions' banter and the music we played on the car's tinny tape player as we drove down from our homes in the Vale of Clwyd. If I really concentrated, I might be able to remember the sandwiches I ate below Adam and Eve.

I imagine that almost all mountain enthusiasts, no matter what stripe, go through a similar early apprenticeship. You don't even realise you are being sucked in, it just happens. I am now well into my 50s and my enthusiasm for the mountains has never dimmed, not even for a month. It is a way of life which never alters in its basic scope, and never loses its appeal. After a certain age it provides not just a feast of memories but a never-ending list of future objectives. Not so much a mid-life crisis, as a whole life crisis.

Within a couple of months of that day in 1988, we were knocking off the harder scrambles like South Gully. And within a year I was climbing mountains in Arctic

Norway on an expedition with new university friends, then beginning the long process of ticking off all of Tryfan's classic rock climbs.

A lifetime in the mountains followed, all of which was sparked in a certain sense by Tryfan. I never rose above the status of 'average climber' (at most) and found myself much more suited to the demands of fell running (and I'm not all that great at that either). But I never lost a genuine love for upward movement on prime Welsh granite, and I still fundamentally believe that the kind of relaxed climbing offered by Tryfan, on accommodating holds and with a sense of pleasure at every turn, is the most natural and enjoyable form of mountain activity.

Like a lot of keen middle-aged outdoor enthusiasts, I have by now climbed thousands of mountains on every continent apart from Antarctica (because I can't afford it), most of them much higher and superficially more impressive, but Tryfan still remains that constant backdrop to life itself. It is never boring, its appeal never fades: it is the perfect mountain.

Owen Glynne Jones

The climbs

It often surprises non-climbers to learn that the famous routes on Tryfan's East Face are regarded as 'easy'. If it is famous for anything in climbing terms, it is for its long straightforward classics which have a strong mountaineering flavour. I'm not sure it ever really had a heyday, in the sense that even in the nineteenth century it was regarded as a less serious playground (when compared, for example, to Lliwedd which is a far more serious piece of rock).

Its reputation as an easy venue for novices and geriatrics is long established, although such snobbery is usually accompanied by the caveat that it is also a really lovely and enjoyable place to climb (or words to that effect). Here is climber C.F. Holland writing about Tryfan in 1948, for example: 'Experts pour scorn on its jug-handle holds and the lavish disposal of soft options, with a walk-off on every ledge; but the average climber wisely takes no notice of these outpourings, and the east face is still the usual objective on a fine day'.

And even Holland concedes that some corners of Tryfan are pretty steep and holdless: 'It is customary to designate Tryfan climbing as easy, and easy it may be under good conditions to parties in training; yet sections abound that yield climbing as arduous and as technically interesting as can be found anywhere.'

To non-climbers, the peculiar mentality and preoccupations of rock climbers means little. For ordinary pedestrians, the mountain as a whole, and the East Face in particular, looks steep and downright hard, even a little scary for the timid. This is certainly the case when approaching along Ogwen from Capel Curig, which – as we have already established – is the correct way to first encounter the mountain. There is something inaccessible and intimating about the view for the casual observer. This is largely because, from a distance, the multiple ledges that make climbing here a relaxed delight are mostly invisible.

But when you're actually on the East Face routes, they rarely feel serious – there is almost always a good hold available, or a resting ledge, and the cracks and spikes offer abundant protection. They are, in climbing parlance, 'friendly' climbs. As a result, climbing here is popular – much more popular than steeper crags with greater levels of cachet and higher levels of technical difficulty.

Mike Bailey's Ogwen climbing guidebook puts it like this: 'Tryfan always gives good value, and some of the finest mountaineering routes in Wales are found here; classic, long climbs of a character where technical difficulty is less important than the satisfaction of climbing to a mountain summit, and the adventures to be had along the way'.

The big three mountaineering routes are so famous that they warrant individual treatment.[3] Each has its own character, and its own identity, and each is regarded as the classic way up the three buttresses. This is where the weird symmetry of Tryfan comes into play again: three buttresses, separated by dark gullies: South, Central, and North. Each of those buttresses houses one classic route that almost all British climbers will have done at least once.

Up the middle and widest buttress is the easiest of the big three: Pinnacle Rib.

This has two distinct, almost separate, variants and goes by a rather confusing variety of names (First Pinnacle Rib, Overlapping Rib Route, and others). It is a beautiful climb, excellent for beginners with good holds and good protection almost throughout. It does have one surprise, however, and it is one of the most famous 'stoppers' in Snowdonia. 'Stopper' being the operative term for a difficult move that causes leaders to slow down considerably as they try to figure it out.

This is the Ochre Slab. Out of character with the rest of the route, it is a beautiful sweep of textured rock, characterised by tiny ripples that give technical and balancey climbing that is far removed from the usual kind of East Face climbing on Tryfan, which generally involves hauling up on extravagant holds. As its name suggests, it has a certain amber glow, which is particularly alluring in the early morning as the low sun lights the face.

Some have said that this little pitch would warrant a much higher technical grade if it was on a harder route. Luckily for our purposes, one or two sketchy

---

[3] *This is not a climbing guidebook, and is not intended to be used as such.*

Above the Ochre Slab on Pinnacle Rib

moves up the ripples gain a bigger hold and then the normal Tryfan East Face service is resumed. Above, a beautiful curving line of flakes leads upwards with big holds all the way.

Then you have a decision to make. Either saunter up to the summit, which is little more than a stroll from here. Or do battle with the legendary Thompson's Chimney, the purist's finish. When I first did Pinnacle Rib as a young whippersnapper, it was a very cold March day – wet snow lying throughout. I seem to remember that the guidebook we used at the time (it was the late 1980s) gave us no choice – it seemed adamant, insistent even, that the chimney was the only possible finish. So we dutifully entered into its wet, cold and slippery clutches, emerging slightly wiser young men.

Returning to Thompson's Chimney much more recently, I was surprised by how hard it was: a real 'thrutch' (a climbing term that needs little translation, generally indicating an unpleasant and inelegant battle to make upward progress). Indeed, it now warrants a higher grade and a warning that it is out of character with the rest of Pinnacle Rib.

There are a few more short climbs up this final wall too – like The Wall and Ghost Chimney. They are also steep, but on excellent rock and rarely ascended.

Moving to the north buttress, the boringly titled 'North Buttress' is another very old climb (first climbed by O G Jones, Abraham and Puttrell in 1899). It takes a pronounced groove rising from the Heather Terrace and was one of the first 'multipitch' climbs I ever did as a teenager, with my friend Tim, the impoverished but proud owners of three or four slings and very little else.

Fortunately, it was, and remains, an easy way up the face (caution is needed at the start, however, as there is a parallel and harder variation start line right next to the shallow, appealing open groove which forms the real, easy start). So easy, in fact, that it is standard to combine North Buttress with the so-called 'Terrace Wall Variant', which weaves gently up that particular feature of the mountain, traversing rightwards in a wonderful position.

This variant is so eye-catching and photogenic that it formed the basis of one of the best known early photographs of rock climbers in action, taken by the famous Abraham brothers of Keswick in the Lake District. There they are, two classic Victorian gentlemen, stretched out across the traverse line with all the necessary ingredients: sepia tinting, tweed jackets, luxuriant moustaches, impractical headgear, pipes.

Nowadays, the Terrace Wall is not often visited, apart from this variant, and another classic climb (graded 'VS' by the traditional British system) that starts from the right-hand side of the wall: Belle Vue Bastion. Although small, the Bastion is perfectly formed, and was apparently recognised as the best route here long before it was actually climbed.

When that day came, the leader was one Ivan Waller, who is said to have led the route to the strains of gramophone music that he had lugged up here from Ogwen: an impressive feat in itself. It is a wonderful story, and probably true. What is definitely true is that Waller came back to repeat the climb 58 years later, his ascent pictured in the Ogwen climbing guidebook of the 1990s.

The route is much shorter than the big mountaineering routes: in fact it only has two pitches. The bottom is the hardest technically, graded 4c, up a delicate groove to the deliciously named 'grove of bollards'. When I climbed the route in 2011, my notes described this as 'a

On the East Face looking up to Belle Vue Bastion

fantastic place with mist swirling around and intermittent views down to Ogwen'. The top is easier but gives the route its reputation as it is highly photogenic. It involves a little skip up to a ledge, and then a delicate and exposed traverse to the right, above something of a void: spectacular but relatively easy with a technical grade of 4b.

There are other climbs on the Terrace Wall, which incidentally is a delightfully sunny place to be, sometimes even above the clouds, particularly in autumn when temperature inversions are relatively common. They are rarely ascended, however, and might be a little dirty if you choose to venture this way.

To give a flavour, after doing one of these routes some years ago (the unimaginatively named 'Linear Climb'), my contemporaneous notes described this as a 'slightly disappointing route, not helped by the fact that it was wet and dirty. A nice groove goes up to a small roof, good moves left avoid the roof to gain a slab, then steep moves on flat holds lead to another groove. The rest of the second pitch looked pointless – a wet, mossy scramble'.

In other words (and it is an important point) there are corners of Tryfan on which you won't see anybody else. Despite the huge popularity of this mountain, it is still big enough to allow for this, and even provides a sense of exploration at times. You might even capture the flavour of the past if you get sufficiently lost.

One of those hidden corners, on the dark side of the South Buttress, houses one of Wales's most infamous climbs. Still known as Munich climb, it was originally climbed by a party of top German climbers who placed three pitons, an incident that affronted the British climbing establishment and became part of climbing folklore. Leaving aside the curious question of why a group of Germans, particularly Bavarians (which I assume they were given the climb's name) were messing around on little pieces of Welsh granite when they live next to the Alps and the peerless Kaisergebirge, this celebrated incident has always seemed to me a tiny bit suspicious.

There is just something about the perfect way the story plays into national stereotypes, allowing the British to claim the moral high ground, something they are generally delighted to do, that I find almost too good to be true. Climbing ethics are a complicated issue, too complicated to discuss here, but suffice to say that the British tradition has always frowned upon the use of fixed protection – this would have been hammered-in pitons or pegs in the past, and is now bolts drilled into the rock.

The ethical purity associated with what is now called 'trad' climbing (by a younger generation) is often presented as symbolic of British superiority, although in reality the paucity of rock in the UK and the small scale of our mountains means that there is a large degree of logic to the differences. Blank limestone walls and committing Alpine mountains will always lend themselves to fixed protection where considerations of ethical purity might come second to the need to remain relatively safe on long, dangerous routes with multiple additional hazards not present in British hills.

Having said all that, it is necessary to park the cynicism, as I have no evidence whatsoever that the story about the Germans on Tryfan is anything other than completely true.

You will not find too many people on these steeper Tryfan walls, they are a little intimidating, far removed from the sun-drenched ease of the gentler mountaineering routes. But they do again illustrate the point that it is possible to find solitude on the mountain, even in the frantic staycationing era in which we now live.

It was more peaceful in the distant past though, of that there is little doubt. Here is Dorothy Pilley writing in the late 1950s, giving a flavour of earlier turn-of-the-century climbing days in Tryfan while rueing the popularity of the post-war era, in her essay 'forty years back': 'In those days before the scratches replaced the footholds, the East Face of Tryfan often felt as if no one had been on it before. Wandering about, linking up ledge with ledge , you would only intermittently know which route you might be on. Then it was: can I get up? Not – has someone been?'

When it comes to the 'big three' most popular mountaineering routes, you are unlikely to be alone. They have been popular since they were first climbed at the end of the nineteenth century, and

Climbing on Terrace Wall

although they have never been at the cutting edge in terms of climbing standards and styles, their appeal endures.

Even back in 1948, C.F. Holland (in the same book as previously quoted) acknowledged its popularity as a climbing venue: 'In spite of the great advance made of recent years in the climbing on the Glyders, and the higher standard of difficulty set by the general use of rubber shoes, Tryfan is still, as it always has been and probably always will be, the great centre of attraction for the majority of climbers who visit the district.'

Holland continues with a few flourishes typical of the time, dealing with a contemporary cliché which stressed the seriousness of climbing on Lliwedd (the large cliff that frames Llyn Llydaw, a familiar sight for the thousands of Snowdon walkers who toil up the Miners or Pyg tracks) before contrasting it with the perceived triviality of Tryfan.

Here is an example: 'The phrase "playing for knuckle-bones with Tryfan before tossing for crowns with Lliwedd" is picturesque, and one for which we have often given thanks, but it needs to be seen in its proper perspective. Tryfan has its music too: the horns of Elfland may be heard calling from its battlements, but the fruits of half-contemptuous attitude towards its difficulties have been a casualty list nearly as heavy as that of Lliwedd itself.'

In a similarly effusive vein, Holland hints that, although less rewarding in mountaineering terms, climbing on Tryfan is simply more fun: 'Old age will be made more serene by the contemplation of achievement and we may then rest happy in the thought that we have earned a place in the climber's Valhalla and the right to climbing up the Golden Steps'.

Whatever, 'fun' is the operative word when it comes to climbing on Tryfan. It is a place for climbers to enjoy themselves, not a place to scare themselves silly or seek to polish their egos and push their grades. That said, those new to the sport (or former rock gymnasts in their dotage) will have certain routes that they want to tick, the most famous classics, the most talked-about routes.

On Tryfan, there is little doubt about the most sought after classics and, unsurprisingly given the previously mentioned triple symmetry of the peak, there is one classic route on each buttress. The big three have – for a very long time – been Pinnacle Rib (which has already been described, as it heads up the central buttress), Gashed Crag (which takes the best line up the south buttress) and Grooved Arete (which does the same up the north buttress).

Gashed Crag was first climbed by Buckle and Barlow in 1902. The crux of the route is an old-fashioned struggle up a chimney, another of those 'thrutches' in climbing terms. Showell Styles took a traditional view of this when writing about the route in the influential coffee table book of climbing essays *Classic Rock* (1978): 'Tiptoeing across the slant of the lower jaw, you sidle round the corner to the foot of a chimney so good and old fashioned that it must gave gladdened the hearts of Buckle and Barlow when they came upon it.' Times have changed, and very few climbers' hearts are nowadays gladdened by the sight of a chimney promising ripped clothing and skin.

Apart from that chimney, Gashed Crag gives climbers the archetypal Tryfan experience, delightful open climbing up delicate aretes and the like. Above, Bubbly Wall gives a superb finish: a little harder but short and on interesting and intriguingly textured volcanic rock, as its name suggests.

Grooved Arete was climbed by a large team containing two famous activists of the day – EW Steeple, and the same Guy Barlow that first climbed Gashed Crag, in 1911. Steeple describes the ascent of what came to be known as 'the Knight's Move', a delicate tiptoe across a slab with small holds, named after the chess piece, as it goes right, then up. 'Near the south end of the Haven [a welcome ledge] a few feet of moderately easy rock and a short grassy cleft gave access to the commencement of this slab. I did not like the look of the place any better on a second inspection, and the credit of the successful issue is due to Woodhead, who came up with a little pick and with infinite patience cleared out a line of small holds up the slab. These run at first to the right, then straight up to a small rock recess, about 50 feet above the Haven'.

With modern footwear and protection, this probably isn't much of a 'crux' any more for most climbers, who may find the groove directly below a little harder. As a climb, however, Grooved Arete remains as it was described in the classic 1980s guidebook, 'the most inspiring and well-known route on Tryfan'. Indeed, it is one of the best 'mountaineering' routes in the whole of Britain and will always be very popular. It transcends fashion and trends, and will be cherished long after the last indoor climbing wall has been demolished. Probably.

There is another famous crag on Tryfan, tucked away on the western side of the foot of the North Ridge and familiar to all motorists passing on the A5 road: the Milestone Buttress. As Tom Leppert said in his classic Ogwen guidebook of the 1980s,[4] 'the Milestone is a very busy buttress. Yet from its comfortable ledges

---

[4] *My copy is so well thumbed that the spine has fallen apart, it was another one of my early bibles, read and re-read until the route descriptions returned to me in my dreams.*

there are always moments when you can gaze across Llyn Ogwen and reflect on more peaceful times.'

Whether traditional cliffs like this, even ones with easy routes, are busier or less busy than they were a few decades ago is a topic of furious debate among climbers. Some say they are less busy, with younger climbers lured away by the safer and more sanitised attractions of climbing walls, bouldering and sunny bolted crags in the Mediterranean. Others disagree. Whatever, the Milestone certainly remains popular, its routes are scoured clean of vegetation after decades of traffic, its holds polished to a high sheen.

The slabby front of the buttress contains several classic easy routes, often the first routes that climbers start their careers on. I was no exception, doing Direct Route with my friend Tim Holt as a callow youth on an icy midwinter day. That route, the Direct, is one of the most frequently climbed in the whole of Snowdonia and alongside Grooved Arete (and perhaps Hope on the Idwal Slabs) is almost certainly the most popular climb in the whole of the Ogwen valley (logged 3246 times on the UKC climbing website by 2022, as opposed to seven ascents of the vastly harder Wrinkled Retainer at the back of the Milestone Buttress, which I am about to mention).

The four pitches of the Direct Route are varied and interesting, encompassing several different climbing styles but remaining simple. Nearby is the even easier Pulpit Route and equally simple Rowan Route, as well as the much harder Superdirect, graded HVS, and taking – as its name suggests – an uncompromising line up the crest of the central ridge.

None of these routes are particularly 'natural' lines, indeed Tryfan is a little light on those sorts of features. At the back of the Milestone, a much less friendly place, dank and dark, lurks one obvious exception: a large curving corner known as 'Soapgut'. It might not surprise the reader to learn that climbing this can be a rather slippery and insecure experience: dry weather is advisable, a severe drought would be optimal. Mike Bailey's modern guidebook to climbing in the Ogwen valley neatly sums it up: 'One of the classic routes of Tryfan... but in greasy conditions only the stout-hearted will succeed'.

The thin crack on the left of Soapgut is 'Crazy Horse', a much harder route climbed by Harwood and Sharp in the

1980s, a decade in which climbing standards soared across the region, often driven by unemployed young men living in Llanberis terraces, or whatever shed or cave they could find for accommodation.

Also near here is arguably the hardest 'proper' climb on Tryfan, the Wrinkled Retainer, currently graded at a hefty E5 6c, *very* hard in other words. Some short pitches scattered around the mountain are harder, including one [called 'Nectar Too'] near the summit and a few other really difficult pitches near this steep part of the Milestone Buttress. These will hardly ever be climbed, they are just too difficult for most climbers.

The Wrinkled Retainer does have a reputation, however, and attracts a certain amount of attention. This is largely because it was the scene of an infamous incident in the annals of Welsh climbing, when a tree (which used to provide an easier start to the route) was cut down, presumably in a misguided attempt to increase the purity of the climb and intensify the climbing. The culprits were then unable to get up the route.

A top climber of the era, John Redhead, was drafted in, unaware of the context –

made the first ascent in good style – and named the route. It so happened that the climber responsible for the original climb, with the tree, was even more famous. He was Martin Boysen, who was part of Chris Bonington's celebrated South-West face of Everest expedition in the 1970s.

Thinking Redhead responsible, Boysen wrote a furious letter to *Crags*, a contemporary climbing magazine: 'Dear Mr Blockhead, I congratulate you on 'creating' the variation start to Desecration Crack – a fine little route which I did with John Yates last year... it was a splendid tree and quite large to be growing in so inhospitable a place... perhaps chain saws will soon be as small and convenient to carry as a large friend' ['friends' are camming devices used in cracks for protection].

The tree has since recovered and, while this might seem like an arcane argument among peculiar climbing enthusiasts, it does touch on some very modern issues and environmental preoccupations: a tree-preservation order should perhaps now be served on it.

over: View of Llyn Ogwen from the foot of Tryfan

The rounds

Tryfan is small. There is no getting away from it. While it might have a grand façade, and it might feel big when you are getting a bit tired near the North Tower, the reality is that even by the standards of these islands, it is not very big – nowhere near 1000 metres, it stands at a mere 918 metres, or 3010 feet, above sea level. This is an issue that all climbers, hillwalkers and fell runners in the UK have a solution to, however. That solution is to combine hills together: the fitter you are, the more you might combine in a single journey.

And in that sense, as well as all the others, Tryfan is perfectly placed. It can form a memorable start, or conclusion, to any number of longer outings in the Welsh mountains.

Arguably the most common combination is with the nearby peaks of the Glyderau: a route often known as the Bochlwyd horseshoe/Pedol Bochlwyd. This is one of the best scrambling days in the UK, and stands comparison with the more famous Snowdon Horseshoe. It is normally done clockwise, starting with the North Ridge from the A5, descending the South Ridge to Bwlch Tryfan, ascending Bristly Ridge on Glyder Fach, which is similar to – although slightly harder and more committing than – the North Ridge.

Then, the scrambler can enjoy a somewhat more relaxed crossing of the Glyder plateau (perhaps pausing for smaller scrambles to the true summit of Glyder Fach, as well as up the Cantilever and perhaps the romantically poised pile of rocks with an equally romantic name, Castell y Gwynt/Castle of the Winds). Half way across the plateau, a rightwards turn gains the top of the Gribin ridge, which gives a mild scrambling descent to Cwm Bochlwyd – after which a stepped descent beside the lake's outflow stream leads back to the A5.

While that is the classic Bochlwyd Horseshoe, it is very common to extend it to take in the higher Glyder Fawr, before descending its fearsome screes to return to Idwal via the intimidating Twll Ddu/Devil's Kitchen, or going even further and taking in Y Garn, another iconic Glyderau peak.

Similarly, remaining in the Glyderau one might choose to seek out the vastly

Tryfan from Caseg Fraith

quieter peaks that lie in the other, easterly direction from Bwlch Tryfan, all of which provide a different perspective on Tryfan. A delightful contouring path leads up to lonely Llyn Caseg Ffraith, for an obvious starting point to continue the day in this direction. This shallow sheet of water, the lake of the speckled mare, repays further exploration as it is one of the best vantage points for the famous view of the East Face.

I camped here on a midsummer's day in 2017, specifically to enjoy the view of Tryfan as the sun set behind it. I took a rather circuitous route, as the weather was perfect: deep blue skies, warm but not hot, Welsh granite at its alluring best. So some rock action seemed the order of the day before settling down to what I hoped would be a memorable evening. My contemporary notes taken at the time give something of the flavour of these trips, of which I try to do a few each year. There is nothing quite like a solo wildcamp to give a sense of full immersion in the Welsh mountain landscape.

A magical overnight trip in perfect conditions, starting late on a Sunday afternoon with all of Ogwen to myself. After a father's day lunch, I didn't set off until almost 5pm, heading straight up towards the upper end of the West Face of Tryfan with temperatures in the high 20s and not a cloud in the sky. I am gradually ticking off the routes on the West Face, none of which will ever be popular, but by judicious combinations the scrambling is almost as continuous as it is on the vastly more popular East.

I'm not sure I'd ever bother coming here with a partner, but on a solo day its relaxed and exploratory vibe is perfect. I had full overnight kit, tent and stove, so needed to select my route carefully: I went for Y Gully, a very obvious line visible from most of Ogwen. The long and gentle stream bed/shallow gully leads directly into this line, which is characterised by three large chockstones. These look innocuous from below, but are slightly problematic, and the route is far better and more enjoyable than I'd expected. Good scrambling up clean rock leads to a runnel leading left over the second chockstone, then excellent and surprisingly steep rock, festooned with jugs, on the left of the third obstacle leads to a clean rib.

I picked my way satisfyingly up the rest of the face to the North Tower, taking a line parallel to Notch Arete (another fine mountaineering route, done with John Boyle a few years ago). By weaving around, this is rock the whole way up. Wonderful views from a deserted Tryfan summit: the clarity of light was, if anything, even better than from Arenig Fawr yesterday. I jogged down the South Ridge to Bwlch Tryfan, then along the contouring line which I'd used to good effect on the Rab Mountain Marathon, to reach my chosen campsite by Llyn Caseg Fraith. I have had this filed away for years as an ideal camping location, and it was nice to finally sample it: a superb spot and a truly magical campsite in this weather. Virtually no wind, cloudless skies, and as near to the midsummer solstice as to make no difference.

The only real issue is that it is a rather boggy area, but I pitched on a raised platform – completely dry – then had a pleasant evening meal before doing some bouldering on the obvious juggy crag below the lake on the Ogwen side, complete with a perfect 'Diff' groove up the centre (which I christened Noodle Groove – because that's what I'd just eaten). A wonderful few hours passed, as the light changed constantly and the sun dropped into the gap between Tryfan and Bristly Ridge, just as I had hoped it would. Nobody was around, just the odd skylark and raven for company. After the sun dropped, the sky turned purple and, eventually, I turned in to read the Guardian's 'Review'.

Then, next morning, the magic continued:

Having watched the sun setting at 10pm last night, I thought it would be nice to see it rise. This, for me, is the key to a good midsummer camp: uninterrupted views to the east and west. To combine that with a bit of shelter from the wind, and nearby running water, is unusual – which is why this site has been on my mind for some time. It was a very peaceful night, with light breezes gently rustling the tent and only the distant trickle of a stream.

I was woken by a very early skylark, a delightful way to rise, so had a cup of coffee in my sleeping bag before running to the nearby summit of Foel Goch to watch the sun rise, dark red, above Llyn Cowlyd and Pen Llithrig y Wrach: memorable, and still well before 5am. Amazing clarity of light for distant views over the Irish Sea and Lancashire coast. I jogged down and sat on a natural rock chair to watch the early sun illuminate the east face of Tryfan as a raven cronked, as if greeting the first rays. After packing up, I ran straight down Bwlch Tryfan and Ogwen back to the car, where I had some porridge before doing a couple of climbs in what I have always known as 'Tin Can Alley' above the Cottage.

There are, of course, an infinite

number of other, bigger days incorporating Tryfan as part of the outing, generally the domain of fell runners. One is the full traverse of the Glyderau from Bethesda to Capel Curig. I ran this with a group of friends in the winter of 2017, with limited daylight. The weather was not ideal, a familiar thick, claggy mist sat low and persistent over the summits. We had arranged to meet Vic Belshaw 'near the Cantilever', giving him an estimated time of arrival. I still remember it being a classic test of hillcraft – could we stick to our timing whilst getting the navigation bang on and making the rendezvous successfully? As Vic's green jacket materialised out of the mist, the answer was a satisfying 'yes', although he was shivering a little by that point.

Tryfan also forms an essential part of the Welsh 3000s, undoubtedly the best known and most historic of all the big Snowdonian walks: in fact, it has an obvious case as the most famous 'big day out' in all the British mountains, in the sense that it is accessible to most hill walkers, not just deranged fell runners. Tryfan gives a particularly arduous descent if it is taken by the standard south to north

3000s route, down the Western Gully all the way to Ogwen cottage – a big ask for knees that have already had quite a battering by this point on the journey from Snowdon summit.

I vividly remember ploughing down here with friends Peter Agnew and Jez Brown as we attempted to set our own personal bests for the 3000s in 2017: the fact that a pie and a drink awaited at the cottage was motivation enough to get down fast while pushing the next obstacle, the horrible direct ascent of Pen yr Ole Wen, to the back of our minds.

A loop around the Glyderau and Carneddau combined, a giant circuit of the Ogwen valley, is a tad harder than the Welsh 3000s and perhaps best reserved for mountain runners. It involves a relentless series of climbs if done properly, keeping religiously to a line across all the summits.

The biggest round of all is the increasingly famous Paddy Buckley, of which Tryfan is an essential part. On its 100 kilometre gigantic loop, taking in 47 summits, Tryfan takes centre stage, although in an outing on this scale, the impact of any individual peak is inevitably limited, which takes us back to the start of this section – the stature of our mountains is relative, there are always infinite ways in which they can be made more challenging, whether that be an ascent of the ultra-technical 'Wrinkled Retainer', or a sub-24 hour traverse of the Paddy Buckley round.

below: Approaching Bwlch Tryfan midway through a running attempt on the Welsh 3000s; over: Tryfan from lower approach slopes to Pen yr Ole Wen

Accidents

Tryfan's lure, combined with its rocky character, and its popularity as a climbing venue, has meant that it has for a long time had a reputation for accidents. It must be said that this is more a function of its popularity and its unusual steepness and abundance of rock (by British standards) rather than anything inherently dangerous. Indeed, Tryfan's granite is generally solid and reliable. Another issue is that inexperienced parties often get confused by the complex topography, typically failing to locate safe descent routes and finding themselves on awkward or exposed ground. Indeed, on several occasions I have been asked for advice by strangers on Tryfan (far more than on any other Welsh peak) and at least twice have led people down the mountain.

I once stumbled across a young Geordie couple lost in the mist in the amphitheatre above North Gully. I was descending from a rock climb with my friend Steve Toogood, and bumped into them in the mist. They were delighted and relieved to see us and immediately asked for help getting down, so we led them to the hard to find (especially from above) Little Gully back to the safety of the Heather Terrace. This was a little out of their comfort zone, as it involves a short section of unavoidable downclimbing, but it is a quick way down, and they eventually reached the terrace unscathed. Our rucksacks were on the Terrace, so we had to go down that way, but it is a perfectly safe route off the mountain if you know the way (perhaps best ascended and fixed in the memory first).

Back in the particular context of the 1950s, CF Holland identified another one of the reasons that climbers sometimes get into trouble on the peak, citing the 'commonly accepted belief' in the innocuous character of this mountain, which leads 'moderate parties to attack its climbs under conditions unsuitable for any but the strongest combinations, forgetful that in the wet, the cold and the snow of winter, or even through mere lack of physical condition, a mere bagatelle in fair weather may become a problem of great difficulty and danger, calling for the skill of the alpine expert combined with a first class rock climbers capacity for maintaining his position in places where the average man would collapse, and where maybe, in addition to this, every member of the party is called on to exhibit the endurance of an arctic explorer.' A slight exaggeration, perhaps, but the main point stands and can, I suppose, be filed under the headline 'hubris'. Familiarity should not breed contempt, and many climbers know from experience that over-confidence can cause problems.

Bob Maslen Jones tells the story of a 1901 incident in which five climbers, Mr and Mrs Chaytor, A. Fontannaz, Percy Weightmann and J.H. Milton, set out from Gwern y Gof Uchaf and headed for the North Gully which they reached at 1.30pm. It was the 7th of April and there had been recent heavy snowfall (snow is more common at Easter than at Christmas, in Snowdonia and elsewhere). Several of the gully's pitches were completely covered in deep snow making for slow progress, as the obstacles in the gully are steep and awkward. They climbed the route successfully, however, although it took them longer than expected.

The weather closed in at the summit and they descended the North ridge in thickening mist. They missed the correct route down and deviated slightly to the right which bought them 50 feet down to the buttress that skirts North Gully (where I stumbled across the young Geordie couple). Seeing a precipitous drop below, they realised their mistake, but rather than climb back to find the true ridge line, they looked for another way down. Weightmann, 'a strong, active and sure-footed climber' disappeared from view after 30 feet. The rest of the party received no reply to their increasingly frantic calls. Milton climbed down and saw the mark of a slip made by Weightmann's boots in the snow. A long way below, 600ft according to the account, they found his lifeless body.

Later that year, Archer Thompson, a Llandudno schoolteacher who pioneered many of the early climbs in Ogwen and elsewhere, climbed up to investigate, and concluded that Weightmann had lost his balance when he stepped on soft snow overlying a tilting slab. The accident, said Archer Thompson, 'was a pure mischance, not due to any blameworthy carelessness, but that it should serve to remind climbers of the advisability of using an ice axe as a probe in such situations'.

His balanced conclusion seems particularly pertinent today, in a climate where so many are eager to pass judgment on mountain accidents often with no knowledge of either the individual circumstances, or the context of mountaineering as a whole. Social media, of course, facilitates this – which is presumably one of the reasons why the Ogwen mountain rescue team continually update an online account of their activities, an account which is factual and calmly descriptive, rarely apportioning blame unless it is deserved (which it sometimes is).

Maslen Jones's fascinating little book about North Wales mountain rescue[5] also relates several incidents from the so-called 'Black Easter' of 1951, where Alpine conditions attracted many to the hills, and mountaineering was in something of a post-war growth period. There was an entire sequence of different accidents across Snowdonia that Easter, which began on Tryfan on Maundy Thursday, with a party of seven descending South Gully.

This is milder than the North Gully, but it is still troublesome in places, particularly in winter conditions. The party carried ropes but were not using them, the gully floor was apparently packed with frozen snow and ice (this is quite rare nowadays on Tryfan, as it requires freeze-thaw cycles that are increasingly uncommon). One of the party, almost unbelievably named Norah Batty, chose to descend the ice-chute in the middle of the gully but slipped and fell 500ft to the bottom where her body was later found. Several more fatal accidents followed over the rest of that Easter weekend in Snowdonia.

There is at least one memorial cross on Tryfan, somewhere near Nor'Nor' gully, which commemorates the aforementioned Percy Octavius Weightmann, apparently a wealthy company director from Bootle, who died climbing nearby in the 1901 accident detailed above (the date is carved into the cross). Generally, this sort of thing is not approved of in the British mountains, certainly not in recent, more environmentally-aware times. In the Alps, it is common to encounter memorials to climbers who have died on various routes, but again it is a reflection of the scale of the mountains, not some inherent callousness or Protestant stoicism that

5   *A Perilous Playground* (*Bridge Books*, 1999)

puts a stop to permanent commemorations in the British mountains. The mountains are just too small and limited in scope for that to be feasible.

Tryfan still sees its fair share of accidents and incidents, of course, although it seems distasteful to outline more recent events of this kind. Proper climbing accidents are much rarer nowadays, a result of vastly improved protection, equipment and information. But people still go astray, people still fall, and they always will. The admirable Ogwen mountain rescue team reckons that around a third of its call-outs involve incidents on Tryfan.

For ordinary hillwalkers, particularly the modern day version that may have no memory of a time before GPS devices and smartphones, the mountain is arguably a more dangerous place now. Following a line of beeping dots on a map, or any kind of pre-loaded GPS route, is not likely to be a recipe for success on Tryfan, and in that respect it is in many ways closer to an Alpine peak, or a mountain on the Isle of Skye, than a typical British Isles hill. The terrain is just too complex for that kind of navigational technology to work well; and a mistake, whether caused by GPS or human error, is likely to quickly lead into difficult and possibly dangerous territory quite quickly, especially in descent – as in the case of the two disorientated Geordies.

A large scale (1:25,000) map is useful, as is a topographic guide, but really exploration on Tryfan depends on some route-finding nous and a high degree of common sense. As we have already established, the ancient advice to not climb up something you won't be able to climb down is apposite.

That said, I am also conscious that too many people are sometimes guilty of over-exaggerating the dangers of British mountains. This is not the Karakorum or Alaska. The A5 is just below, nobody is going to starve to death and, in fact, one of the great dangers of the British mountains, hypothermia – usually caused by that lethal but common combination of rain and wind – is, I would suggest, rather less likely on such an accessible peak because you probably won't be lost for long enough to succumb.

But there are a lot of trip hazards, and there are an awful lot of crags to fall off, large and small. The sheer popularity of Tryfan also poses its own problems: many accidents in the mountains are caused by other humans, knocking rocks down from above and the like. Danger certainly lurks for the unwary, and a quick glance at the Ogwen Valley mountain rescue website will quickly confirm this. The website generates a map of incident locations, and a high proportion of these are on Tryfan, every year.

This, from August 2022, is typical: 'While ascending Tryfan North ridge a young walker took a 10-15m tumbling fall hurting their back. A casualty party was deployed to assess the cas and R936 was also requested to investigate the possibility to winch the cas. The team doctor assessed the casualty and a decision was made to attempt to walk them off with assistance. Additional team members and RAF MRT were also deployed with stretcher and ropes in case of TRR extraction while 936 was stood down. After a further slip on the descent the casualty was placed on a confidence rope and assisted back to Oggie Base'.

Or this, from the same month. 'A walker called to say that they had become cragfast on the eastern side of Tryfan after having turned back from their planned route and straying down on to steep ground. A small party of 3 were deployed up the Heather Terrace path to locate the walker and a spotter was placed in Gwern Gof Isaf campsite from where they were able to identify the cas just below the Haven. The hill party met the walker and short roped them down Little Gully and onto Heather Terrace before descending back to the road.'

In fact, to continue this mini-exemplar, the Ogwen team recorded ten incidents on Tryfan in this month, August 2022, alone.

There are also a lot of the sorts of incidents that involve a panicked call from individuals lost, confused or stuck, which would not have occurred in the days before mobile phones. Again, these are all from that one summer month, plucked at random, August 2022.

'An informant called to say that they were descending Tryfan but had become stuck on steep ground and they were now feeling unwell and vomiting. With limited light left the Coastguard Helicopter R936 was tasked to assist as the casualties' location was not confirmed. They were located in the Milestone Buttress area and winched off back to Oggie Base and advised to take themselves to hospital for assessment.'

And this, from two months earlier: 'A walker staying at a campsite in the valley decided to go for a low level afternoon walk but followed tracks which took them up into steep ground on the west face of Tryfan. Unable to continue up or descend they called for help and an initial hill party was deployed. The walker was located in the Wrinkle Tower area on the west face of Tryfan and assisted back to easier ground and then down the North Ridge and back to the road.'

It seems important to avoid the obvious cliché about technology being both 'blessing and curse', but it is impossible not to succumb. The British approach to mountain rescue has always been voluntary, in the sense that the crews are all volunteers: highly skilled and committed, but volunteers all the same. The wider public, and more importantly the media, often misunderstands this reality in their rush to judge ill-prepared hill-goers. To continue the Alpine analogies already made, the approach there is very different, with professional rescue services and insurance a necessity. Again, however, this is a logical concession: a climbing accident on an Alpine North Face has very different implications to a fall on Tryfan.

The problem comes when that voluntary system is abused, often by people new to the mountains who have little appreciation of the traditional approach to mountain rescue in the British Isles. Anecdotally, this seems to have worsened during the staycation boom that followed the Covid lockdowns, with many people 'discovering' the Welsh mountains for the first time but lacking even basic understanding of the upland environment. Recent tales abound of walkers requesting helicopter rescues because they are too tired, or have twisted an ankle, and so on.

over: Sunset behind Tryfan from east

The people

The land around Tryfan, and indeed most of the land in Ogwen, has never had a large human population. The climate is too harsh, for one thing, and the slate industry developed lower down Nant Francon around Bethesda. That vibrant Welsh-speaking town remains as characterful and distinctive as it ever was, in contrast to the seemingly empty upper reaches of Ogwen around Tryfan.

There was no slate to be found in Ogwen itself, and there is little evidence of mine workings throughout the valley, which is quite unusual in the context of Snowdonia. Mining still impacts the landscape around Tryfan, however, with the old Miner's Track that leads up Cwm Tryfan over the low boggy shoulder near Llyn Caseg Fraith between Glyder Fach and Foel Goch. This then leads down to the copper mines of Yr Wyddfa/Snowdon. This is an exception, however, and it becomes clear when examining the large scale Ordnance Survey map that there is little archaeological evidence of past settlement.

People have always visited the area surrounding Tryfan, of course. Geraint Roberts relates an ancient story of Welsh princes hunting around Bochlwyd below the mountain. An old grey buck was harried to the point of exhaustion by the hounds when it reached the edge of a small cliff above the lake (of which there are plenty). As the dogs closed in for the kill, it leapt into the cold waters of the lake and managed to escape. Certainly, there are numerous references to the area around Bochlwyd being used by noblemen for their hunting, and Roberts says that arrowheads have been found on the Tryfan slope of the lake.

Further to the point, it is notable that there are several 'animal' place-names across the Glyderau. The names are so ancient that they are lost in the mists of time, but it is possible to speculate, in an educated way, about their origins. Llyn Caseg Fraith, which provides one of the finest views of our mountain, translates as the lake of the speckled mare. Filiast, further along the range, is greyhound. Cywion, which gives its name to a crag on the slopes of Y Garn, translates as 'chicken', or perhaps (given the context) grouse.

Llyn y Cwn, below Glyder Fawr, is a better known example of the same phenomenon, which Condry suggests points to memories of an ancient hunting and pastoral way of life.[6] He also speculates that the modern-day campers seen around Llyn Bochlwyd are possibly

Gwern Gof Isaf

the first people to live, however temporarily, in that cwm below Tryfan since the days of Bronze Age man.

Condry admits there is no direct evidence that Bronze Age people did live

---

[6] *In medieval times there was a royal hunting forest in Snowdonia, at least according to John Leland, who is quick to observe that 'forest', in earlier times, referred not to a tree-covered place but an open, mountainous landscape populated by boar, deer and other animals driven up from the trees onto open ground.*

below Tryfan, but adds that 'it would be strange if they did not – for Cwm Bochlwyd, with its deep clean lake and its mighty encircling cliffs is one of the truly magnificent retreats of Snowdonia'.

However, there are also clues to a somewhat more 'real' past, and it is a relatively recent past. Consider, for example, the tiny chapel of Nant y Benglog, supposedly the highest chapel in Wales, nestling in the valley below our mountain. It is also one of the smallest congregational chapels, built in 1853 by locals who did not want to travel to their places of worship, a perfect illustration of the realities of life in upper Ogwen in the past. Upland chapels like this point to larger populations which, although scattered, would have contributed to a more vibrant rural culture.

It is an unforgiving environment, of course. Occasionally, in the harder winters of the past, snow would fill the interior of the Nant y Benglog through cracks in the masonry (the chapel was constructed from local stone, which is of course abundant). A crowd of 800 attended its centenary in 1953. Now it stands as a rather sad reminder of another era in the valley, one in which a genuinely local population eked out a living.

The road below, which is now the busy A5, was supposedly originally built by the obnoxious Lord Penrhyn to link his inland estates at Capel Curig with Penrhyn quarry and his even more considerable estates on the coast near the stately home: now a famous National Trust property. Given the history of this individual, it seems likely this was predominantly a self-serving initiative as opposed to an attempt to facilitate ease of movement for locals, let alone democratise access to the Welsh hills.

It was never considered a particularly easy route, although given the nature of Snowdonia's topography the actual line of travel through Ogwen and Nant Francon has presumably served a function as a through route, an obvious low-level pass through the mountains, for millennia. It was later famously modified by Thomas Telford who built his more evenly graded London to Holyhead road through the same gap in the mountains, one of the engineer's most celebrated achievements.

The old road is still there, however, and for the most part runs parallel to the A5 down Ogwen and then down Nant Ffrancon: you do not need to look very hard for it. In fact, the only place where it is indetectable is the stretch between Tryfan and Ogwen Cottage, presumably because there is literally only one way through this stretch of land between Llyn Ogwen and the craggy valley side, and the modern A5 roars right through that narrow space. The old route in its entirety is now an enjoyable way of traversing the valley down to Nant Ffrancon, well away from the noise of the main road: a particularly good option if foul weather forces you off Tryfan, or any other Ogwen mountain, onto a lower route.

George Borrow travelled along this road in the 1860s, and the resultant encounters form a long section of his celebrated travel book 'Wild Wales'. Much has been written about Borrow, and the idiosyncratic book, but suffice to say that he manages for the most part to be simultaneously remarkably arrogant and endearingly respectful (he makes great play of his abilities in self-taught Welsh). These encounters, as he approaches Tryfan, are typical of his style, as he demands answers from bewildered locals, who are presumably confused by what was likely to be his rather outré pronunciation (he was from Norfolk).

As he approaches Tryfan, he sees a 'wretched hovel' (since the 1920s, a famous climbing hut) and sees two children looking over a low wall.

'Have you any English?' said I, addressing the boy in Welsh.

'Dim gair,' said the boy; 'not a word; there is no Saesneg near here.'

'What is the name of this place?'

'The name of our house is Helyg,'[7]

'And what is the name of that hill?' said I, pointing to the hill of the precipice.

'Allt y Gog – the high place of the cuckoo.'

This may have been a misunderstanding on Borrow's part: the mountain is actually called Gallt yr Ogof, which frames the view of Tryfan from the east.

Borrow later tells the children that they look unwell. They reply that they have lately had the ague, of which they say there is 'plenty' locally, but that 'when we have bread we live well'. Lower down, he falls into conversation with another man as

---

[7] *Still the name of the Climbers Club hut, which retains its character.*

they pass below Tryfan. The man is so delighted to have found an Englishman who speaks Welsh that he enters two or three cottages by the side of the road to tell the inhabitants. 'It will be a thing to talk of for the rest of my life', says the man. 'I am with a Sais who can speak Cymraeg'.

The author did have a tendency towards exaggeration, but these encounters, and the obvious existence of numerous pedestrians, hovels and cottages along the Ogwen valley below Tryfan, give a nicely contemporary picture of earlier times in the valley below Tryfan.

Given the less than glorious reputation of many of the landlords who owned swathes of the Welsh uplands in the past, it seems pertinent to pose the following question: who actually owns Tryfan? The answer is reassuring. The mountain is now held in perpetuity by the National Trust, who purchased the 21,000 acres of the Glyderau, including Tryfan, from the aforementioned Penrhyn estate in 1951.

There are eight tenant farms scattered across this parcel of land. The closest farm to Tryfan itself is Gwern y Gof Uchaf, although its neighbour Gwern y Gof Isaf is probably better known to most visitors, and has been used by generations as 'base camp' for assaults on Tryfan. The farm has been owned and worked by the Williams family for eight generations, and the campsite was launched by the entrepreneurial Jane Williams (who the family still refer to as 'Hen Nain' [great grandmother]) in 1906.

In contrast to the widely admired Jane Williams, the first Baron Penrhyn – Richard Pennant – is less fondly remembered locally, despite his links with the building of the A5 road. The Pennants traced their roots back to an old Flintshire family and made their fortune through slavery, owning Jamaican sugar plantations since the seventeenth century. Richard Pennant invested the ill-gotten Jamaican profits in Snowdonia, setting up the Penrhyn slate quarry and numerous agricultural estates, as well as building roads, houses and the like. Both he, and his cousin to whom the estate passed, always opposed the emancipation of slaves. When that brutal trade was finally abolished, they received a huge amount of compensation for their Jamaican estates, sinking it back into the Welsh quarries, which they exploited largely for their own profit.

Even after the abolition of slavery, the family line continued to demonstrate their unpleasantness, opposing the developing trade union movement and managing the local slate quarries in an overbearing and iniquitous fashion. This led to the bitter strike of 1900-1903, after which there was so much local hatred of the family that they preferred to stay at their other estate in Northamptonshire.

Tryfan today, and indeed the whole of Ogwen, is a nice riposte to the iniquities of past times. With the land owned by the National Trust, rather than the Pennant family, it is there for the nation to enjoy. And enjoy it they do, in their tens of thousands. So the 'people' associated with the mountain now really are *the people*, in the sense that our enjoyment of this mountain is entirely democratic. We can all visit it whenever we want.

Descent to Ogwen from Tryfan

Flora and fauna

On the face of it, Tryfan does not seem a likely place for an abundance of wildlife. There is just too much rock and not enough water for it to provide much of a haven for birds, insects or mammals. Appearances can be a little deceptive, however, because although you are unlikely to encounter much on brief visits to the mountain, in the context of Snowdonia (and British mountains in general) Tryfan is actually somewhat more diverse, and is certainly closer in appearances to the natural biome, the climatic climax vegetation of these islands, than most of its neighbours.

What does this mean in practice? Well, for example, there is more 'heath' on Tryfan than on most of the surrounding peaks, largely because of its steep rocky character, which means grazing pastures have historically been lower on this peak than those of other Ogwen mountains, which tend to be grassier and gentler, considerably less craggy. Heather and other heath flora indicates a more natural ecosystem than the all-too-familiar overgrazed grassland that characterises much of our upland scenery, which creates a landscape that environmental writer and campaigner George Monbiot describes as 'sheepwrecked'.

Monbiot's controversial view maintains that our upland landscape is massively denuded, destroyed largely by sheep farming and overgrazing (in Wales), and also by grouse shooting and deer stalking elsewhere. This sort of grassland is present on many other Snowdonian mountains, so the scraggy heath and rock mix on Tryfan renders the mountain a 'wilder' place, closer to the natural ecosystem than most Welsh mountains. Whatever one's views on sheep farming, it is hard to argue with the central fact that Tryfan does feel like a more natural environment than the Carneddau, which stretch out from the opposite side of the Ogwen valley, for example. On the Carneddau, progress is easy – as any fell runner will tell you – mile upon mile of gently rolling 'moorland'. On Tryfan, progress is less easy: it's not just the rocks, it is also the heather, the flora clinging to the slopes that makes life a little less straightforward for humans, but arguably more diverse in terms of the wild ecosystem.

It is grazed, albeit mainly by goats, as opposed to sheep. There is a small herd of feral goats at large on the mountain, and they have been there for many years, thriving on the inhospitable combination of terrain and its meagre grazing options. The feral goat herd actually belongs to the previously mentioned Williams family from the farm of Gwern Gof Uchaf, directly below Tryfan to the east. They were, apparently, released in the 18th century after wigs (which used goat hair and must therefore have been remarkably uncomfortable and unhygienic) became unfashionable.

William Condry, in his classic work on Snowdonian wildlife, describes the goats

Carneddau from the summit

as an interesting relic of the farming scene of several centuries ago. Shepherds looked on them favourably, he suggests, because they are so much more agile than sheep and therefore graze on dangerous ledges, removing tempting morsels from the eyes of the less agile sheep, who might otherwise have fallen to their deaths.

In 1803, William Hutton made a wildly inaccurate observation, and an even more inaccurate prediction about the goats, and fused it to an equally inaccurate prediction about the Welsh language: 'This old and once numerous inhabitant of Wales, like the language, is declining; and like that, will come to a period.' But the goats, like the language, survive and thrive.

Cloud inversion and heath landscape

There are birds here, but you have to look hard to find them. The wren, with its explosive song, which always seems impossibly loud given its size, is perhaps the most common. This is perhaps because the species has the ability to see out the worst of the winter weather by hiding in tiny crevices and thus thrives in places like Tryfan, which has more tiny wren-friendly nooks than you can shake a stick at. It does suffer in extreme weather, however.

Meadow pipits, the ultimate 'little brown job' of the Welsh uplands, can be seen – although they are nowhere near as numerous here as they are on the gentler peaks across the valley. You might see wheatear or stonechat, although again the habitat is less optimal than on neighbouring peaks. There is always the chance of a surprise, however, as Tryfan is a relatively isolated peak plonked in the middle of the Ogwen valley and therefore something of an obstacle in the midst of a natural thoroughfare.

A dunnock was apparently seen and heard on the very summit of Tryfan in September 1967, according to Condry's other great work, *The Natural History of Wales*. What brought a hedge sparrow (another name for the same species), which is among the most suburban of birds, up to sing on such an inhospitable peak, wondered Condry, before concluding: 'All we can say is that this was an extreme example of a tendency that is fairly common among widely different lowland birds – immediately after the breeding season some of them take to the hills, if only to the lower slopes, attracted by the many summer insects as well as by ripening bilberries and various seeds.'

Even further back in the records, a twite was recorded carrying food on Tryfan in early August 1944. This might not seem significant, but the summer date implies that breeding took place. I have never seen twite on Tryfan, and it is an increasingly rare bird in general, even in its traditional Snowdonian strongholds – which are nearby but lower down. I have seen twite in Nant Francon, and below Braich ty Ddu, and at the bottom of Y Braich, the long ridge that descends from Pen yr Helgi Du. But I have never seen one on Tryfan.

In autumn, perhaps flying east up the Ogwen valley, flocks of winter thrushes like fieldfare and redwing might be seen overhead, along with smaller birds that also form flocks at the end of summer, like chaffinches and perhaps brambling. These sorts of movements are inconspicuous, however, so keep your eyes and ears open.

If those movements are inconspicuous, the ubiquitous herring gulls are the polar opposite: hugely conspicuous, noisy and extrovert. As with other Snowdonian summits, and all Welsh coastal resorts, these birds will snaffle your scotch eggs as soon as your back is turned, and sometimes even when it isn't. They specifically target bald men, apparently, seeing them as potentially vulnerable, so if you are anything like me, wear a hat and try to look tough.

The quintessential bird of the Welsh mountains is the raven: cigfran, 'meat crow', in Welsh. As is often the case with bird names, the Welsh is more precisely observed and usefully descriptive than the English counterpart. Their population has increased considerably in recent years, as they are no longer persecuted as they once were. They nest in rocky areas, often at mid-height in Snowdonia, partly because they breed very early (February to May) and therefore will avoid the very high cliffs of the region and the associated likelihood of bad weather at a crucial time for the chicks. The raven is a wonderful bird, absolutely of its place, its characteristic 'cronk' echoing round the rocks and high summits. For me, the call of the raven is one of the key sounds of the Welsh mountain environment. And when I hear it elsewhere, on an Alpine peak for example, it always reminds me of home.

Lower down, on the shores of Bochlwyd, common sandpiper occasionally do their bobbing-up-and-down thing. The blue riband species, however, is the ring ouzel. A bird of wild places, of open rock and scree, they can sometimes be seen and heard in the rocky, hostile terrain around Bwlch Tryfan. They are a fascinating species, sometimes called the mountain blackbird (mywalchen y mynydd in Welsh), with a distinctive and diagnostic white band around their necks. They migrate to North Africa and Spain for the winter, and return to our mountains every April. The best time to encounter them is probably May, when their clear song, rather like an abbreviated blackbird, resonates in empty high cwms like this, reverberating from the rock.

Choughs sometimes pass through,

although despite their reputation (and that of their close cousins the Alpine Chough, seen in huge numbers in higher continental mountains), they are not very hardy and are more common on the coastal cliffs of Anglesey where the climate is milder. There are a few butterflies, like the common heath and, as ever, a complex selection of tiny moths, but specialist knowledge is generally required for positive identification.

Apart from the goats, and the few birds that eke out a living here or temporarily pass through, animal life is notable by its absence on Tryfan. Referring to the Glyderau in general, Condry recorded common shrews, field voles and a fox at various times, while noting that 'animal life, especially vertebrate life, is naturally sparse along so exposed a ridge'. He quotes an earlier naturalist called Forrest, who found a dead hedgehog at 2,500ft,

suggesting that it was probably carried up here by a buzzard or raven.

Llyn Bochwlyd, nestling in its glacial cwm below, supposedly provides a home to good quality trout. Geraint Roberts cites numerous sources which agree, and suggests that the previously mentioned Lord Penrhyn (a keen angler) stocked the lake with Loch Leven trout from Scotland towards the end of the nineteenth century. The rights now belong to the Ogwen Valley Angling Association, but it is not restocked.

The flora, from lower slopes to the summit rocks is similar, rather denuded. However, according to the peerless authority Condry the enthusiast might identify species like woolly-fringe moss, haircap moss, yellow lichens, some thrift, starry saxifrage, stiff sedge, bilberry, cowberry, crowberry and least willow.

over: Feral Tryfan mountain goats

The seasons

It is rare to see Tryfan plastered in snow. Its general steepness, its heathery ledges and rocky steps, means that it takes a big dump indeed for this to happen. Of course, such conditions are increasingly rare these days but even when winter does hit hard (as it last did in 2010 and 2013) Tryfan tends to be somewhat less popular for winter outings than some of its neighbours. It is certainly not an ideal venue for ice climbers, for fairly obvious reasons. Ice climbing requires frozen water and frozen turf, the sort of thing provided in Wales by Ysgolion Duon (the Black Ladders, high up in Cwm Llafar above Bethesda) or the back of Cwm Idwal. Dank, damp, vegetated, messy north-facing crags are needed, in other words, not the clean lines and sunny faces of Tryfan.

That said, the gullies and ridges do sometimes solidify in a hard winter and become challenging and rewarding ascents. I can remember doing the North Ridge in full winter conditions in 1998, Llyn Ogwen completely frozen below (itself a rare sight), looking like something from Svalbard or Alaska. The ridge is tricky in these conditions, as indeed it can also be when merely snow covered, a much more common phenomenon. In fact, it is hard to take precautions in those more standard conditions of a shallow layer of soft snow – crampons and axes will not do you much good. Instead, a circumspect approach is best.

'Full winter conditions', even before the current warming trend, are fairly rare in the Welsh mountains. On Tryfan, full conditions would mean a period of alternating freeze-thaw-freeze which would render the gullies properly climbable and the ridges genuinely challenging. What is much more common, as previously stated, is a mere covering of soft fresh snow, which is not the same thing.

In addition to all this, and pre-dating the warming trend, is the sheer changeability of the weather in all seasons. This is such a clichéd observation about Snowdonia, and indeed the entire British upland landscape, that it is almost not worth making (and, in fact, recent years have all seen prolonged periods of high

Tryfan and Glyderau from Pen yr Ole Wen

pressure in all four seasons). Whatever happens in the future, however, the underpinning reality is that the weather is changeable.

Whilst this can be frustrating for climbers and hillwalkers, it also has implications for flora and fauna. As Condry observed 40 years ago: 'Perhaps from nature's viewpoint the most trying feature of Welsh mountain weather is not the excessive rain, the occasional attack of deadly cold nor the rare summer heat-wave: it is simply its changeability. An average summer is a rapid alternation of cool wetness and warm sunshine; and in a typical winter a few mild days follow stretches of frosty days all through from November to May'.

Tryfan from lower slopes of Pen yr Ole Wen

He wrote this in 1981 but it still holds true, albeit with a higher likelihood of longer summer heat-waves and a lower likelihood of winter cold snaps. More consistent warmth in summer is already affecting our wildlife, of course, and it remains to be seen what the effect of this might be on the higher Welsh peaks like Tryfan.

One of the hottest days I have experienced in 40 years in the Welsh mountains came in the summer of 2022. Strangely enough, this was not on the day that the Welsh temperature record was broken (that was the 37.1C registered on the 18th of July in Hawarden, near where I live). It was a couple of weeks after that, on a day of very high humidity, no breeze and – obviously – hot sunshine. It was almost as if the drawn-out nature of the heatwave had stored its energy in the rocks themselves as I made my way up the South Ridge as part of an anticlockwise loop around the Cwm Bochlwyd horseshoe.

I have no idea what the air temperature was, but the bottom part of the ridge was by far the hottest: as if the natural amphitheatre formed by the wall of Glyder Fach on one side, and the south side of Tryfan on the other, had combined with the open nature of the landscape around Bwlch Tryfan to generate a natural oven effect.

It reminded me of Wadi Rum in Jordan, or the White Mountains of Crete, or Utah. Heat seemed to radiate off the bare rock, and – as most Snowdonian visitors will know – there is very little vegetation or grass on this high col, and certainly very little shade when ascending from the south. On Tryfan itself, as we have already established, there are no real streams, certainly not in the hot days of summer.

In these conditions, big days in the mountains can descend into a desperate battle against dehydration. On this particular day, I had no need to continue so descended down to the valley in search of water. On other occasions, when doing long mountain races like the Welsh 1000 metre peaks race of 2021, for example, or the even harder Pedol Peris in the late summer of 2008, dehydration has reduced me to a devastated crawl, white-faced and limping.

Coda

All mountains have a sense of permanence, of course, despite the realities of geological time. But if we reduce that sense of permanence to the microscopic slither of time that represents a human life, I suspect most hillgoers will share my view of Tryfan as a constant, a backdrop to life itself.

I cannot remember a time before it. And if, at some point in the future, physical decay prevents me escaping the mundanities of life by scrambling yet again up the North Ridge, or ploughing up the Heather Terrace, or making a speed attempt on the Direct, or ambling up the relaxing pitches of First Pinnacle Rib? Well, I don't know. Will I be content to gaze at the peak from Gwern y Gof Uchaf, picking out the line of Belle Vue Bastion or reliving those early ascents of Gashed Crag or Grooved Arete? I don't know.

It has always been there, for me and for all lovers of the Welsh mountains. Its accessibility means a mini-adventure awaits, seconds away from the A5. And no matter how familiar it becomes, that familiarity never breeds contempt, and there are always new, obscure corners to discover.

You might not be able to get to the Alps, Norway and Rockies, but you will always have Tryfan. Indeed, this became very clear when restrictions eased after the various Covid lockdowns. Where did most people head? The sense of release, of liberty, was palpable – and there was only one way to celebrate.

Whatever the future holds, that stegosaurus profile will still be there, waiting for you as you round the corner from Capel Curig. The three buttresses rising from the Heather Terrace, the gullies dark and defining, Adam and Eve on the summit, the sun dropping behind the North Ridge.

Bibliography

Ashton, Steve (1992) *Scrambles in Snowdonia*

Bailey, Mike (2010) *Ogwen, Climbers' Club Guide*

Barnes, John (1997) *The Birds of Caernarfonshire*

Bingley, William (1798) *A tour round North Wales*

Borrow, George (1862) *Wild Wales*

Carr, Herbert, and Lister, George (1948) *Mountains of Snowdonia*

Condry, W.M. (1966) *The Snowdonia National Park*

Condry, W.M. (1981) *The Natural History of Wales*

Jones, Iwan Arfon (1993) *Ogwen and Carneddau, CC Guide*

Leppert, Z (1982) *Ogwen, CC Guide*

Maslen-Jones, Bob (1998) *A Perilous Playground*

Millward, Roy, and Robinson, Adrian (1978) *Landscapes of North Wales*

Perrin, Jim (2016) *The Hills of Wales*

Poucher, Walter (1962) *The Welsh Peaks*

Roberts, Geraint (1995) *The Lakes of Snowdonia*

Wilson, Ken (1978) *Classic Rock*

Williams, John Ll., and Williams, Lowri (2022) *Hanes Dyffryn Ogwen (website)*

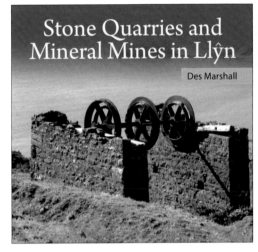
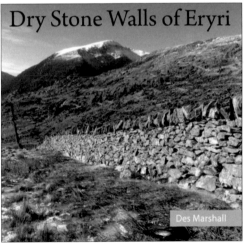

Snowdonia's Waterfalls

Des Marshall

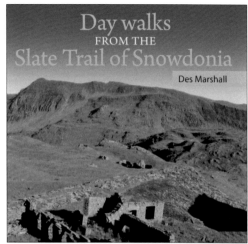

Day walks
FROM THE
Slate Trail of Snowdonia

Des Marshall

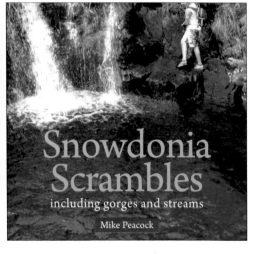

Snowdonia Scrambles

including gorges and streams

Mike Peacock

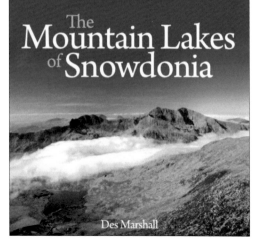

The Mountain Lakes of Snowdonia

Des Marshall

NANT Y BENGLOG, TRYFAN, CWM IDWAL

CYFLWYNIAD | FOREWORD
GERALLT PENNANT